Ramson Lomatewama

SILENT WINDS

poetry of one Hopi

Acknowledgements
Some of these poems have appeared in the following:
The Clouds Threw This Light (Institute of American Indian Arts, 1983)
SPAN (United States Information Service, 1986)
Christian Science Monitor
New Canadian Review

Library of Congress # 83-61654
ISBN 0-935825-00-2

Photography by Sam Minkler

FOURTH EDITION
Printed in the United States of America

Mirror Images — Flagstaff, Arizona

Badger Claw Press
6693 N. Snowflake Drive
Flagstaff, Arizona 86004

For my children

my wife

and those who will follow.

R.R.L.

The author wishes to thank the Heard Museum for its continued support and cooperation in promoting education through the arts.

Special thanks go to the Flinn Foundation of Phoenix, Arizona who made the Artist on the Road program possible, and for their commitment "to improve the quality of life for the people of Arizona".

The Fourth Edition is made possible by The Dr. and Mrs. Dean Nichols Publication Fund, The Heard Museum, Phoenix, Arizona.

CONTENTS

SILENT WINDS

poetry of one Hopi

A CASUAL ACQUAINTANCE

I'm struggling to

carry an armload

of sweet

fresh

corn... still moist

from the last rain.

A bullsnake

taking refuge

curled around

the coolness

of a

strong

corn plant.

Our eyes meet.

I walk past.

Neither of us says

"hello".

IN THE CORNFIELD AT 5:30 AM

The sunflower sways
in the early summer breeze
while the swallow sings
to the coming sun.

The daylight
slowly climbs the horizon
while the bullfrogs
turn and scurry
into the tall
slender cattails.

The crow is awake
and greets the morning.

CAW! CAW! CAW!

Its smooth body shimmering
reflects the sunlight
tis' a black mirror
that circles above.

A rabbit looks quietly
for the shade of grass
as the sun heats
the drying sand.

This morning
I too
greet the dawn.

PURIFICATION DANCE

Ho!
Cloud!

      You carry rain.

Look down upon us
and cleanse all life.

      Show us your happiness

and dance in the sky.
Dance above our cornfields and shower us
                    with rain.

Ho!
Wind!
      You weave above us.
      Is cloud your partner?

She follows your movements.

You dance all night.

      When do you go home?

ANIMAL SPIRIT PRAYER

Toward the south
is antelope mound.

It is a spirit home.

In midst of winter
before sunrise
young men pray.

Desiring that the rabbit
                    fox
                    deer
                    elk

        be plentiful.

A prayer feather
planted in moist
snowcrust earth

carries the prayer

to the animal spirits.

DEER DANCE

Delicate hoofs
        dancing on sacred ground.
Bells and rattles
        make falling-rain sounds
Pounding drumbeat
        calling to the thunder.
Singing clowns
        give life to our prayers.

The dance of the deer

                brings rain.

THE CLOUD PEOPLE SPEAK

Let us depart!

Let us depart
over yonder
to the homes
of our fathers
who have been praying
silently
for our arrival!

Let us depart
with gentle rain
and carry it
in our gourds.

Let us travel
by thunder

by lightning

and by the fullness of the clouds

        above
        fields of corn and squash
        and valleys
        and over mesas.

Let us depart!

Let us depart!

They await our arrival!

WUPATKI

Ancient red stone
jagged silhouette
    rotting mortar

        These are the walls I saw.

Crumbling city
your strength is waning
defeated by the years.

            I see your slow

                    slow

                    death.

How many clans
        seasons
        children
    generations   have you seen?

How many more
will come to pass

before your last stone
has no more life

and you
are unable to see.

DARK HORIZONS

The grey clouds were as mountains
that towered beyond the horizon.
They suffocated the dawn
under the crushing weight
of their darkness!

They brought the merciless wind
that pelted the dogs with grit!

    (making them howl)

They brought the jagged lightning
that butchered the morning sky!

The windows in the houses
echoed the rumbling
of the insane thunder!

They came with the fury
of angry men!

But left us

with life giving

rain.

WINTER SPIRITS

Midnight
and it is kyaamuya
the month of reverence.

   The sandstone walls
   are cold
   and rough to the touch.

      The alleys
      are dead
      and silent.

      The full moon
      casts a blanket of gray.

      Winter spirits

      are hiding in the shadows.

SEASONS

Winter.
Cold dawn.

Somewhere
young eagles cry
still white
and too young to fly.
Rabbit tracks
as if chasing one another
leave spots of water
in the snow.
Icicles cling
to bare peach trees.

Short days.
Long nights.

Orion takes the path of the sun.

Spring.
Warm dawn.

Apple trees
blossom pink.
Hummingbirds
dart in and out
through patches
of wild spinach.
Washes gushing forth
spring floods.
Tumbleweeds conquering
empty cornfields.
Young lambs
wailing in the corrals.
Little boys
making slingshots.

Orion submitting to the sun.

Summer.
Early dawn.

Golden silk
caresses young corn.
Red ants
struggle
to carry their spoils.
Jet
black
stinkbugs
wander aimlessly.
Grey horned toad
stares motionless
frozen in the heat.
Coleman lanterns
invaded by moths.
Drunks fighting by moonlight.

Long days.
Short nights.

Orion rests and no longer travels.

Fall.
Late dawn.

Dust storms
forever swirling.
Crows spiral
high overhead.
Cornstalks
dry
and dead.
Tumbleweeds
guided by the wind.

The sun submitting to Orion.

A RAIN SONG

blue butterfly maiden
yellow butterfly maiden

they chase one another through the cornfield
they chase one another throughout the day

they are happy

from the west
the rain will come

from the east
the rain will come

blue corn maiden
yellow corn maiden

they grow throughout the cornfield
they grow through the day

they are happy

A SHORT SONG
(haiku)

Forest beyond. Thick
          with the aroma of sap.
Thick sap.   Medicine.

IN A MOMENT OF GRIEF

Qalatoto   baby of the earth
             I have disturbed
             your journey.

Qalatoto   Foolishly have I
             ripped you from the womb
             of the moist earth
             and cast you upon the ground!

Qalatoto   you curl in anguish
             from the hot sun
             and the burning sand.

Qalatoto   baby of the earth
             forgive me.
             I know not
             what I do.

WORDS OF WISDOM

Hear me
my nephew.

Let not my words pass
as the wind passes
through the trees.

Let not my words
have no meaning
like the moth who has no soul.

    Listen!
    as your father the fox listens
    for he is strong of courage
    yet quiet of heart.

    Listen!
    absorb my words into your heart
    as our mother the earth
    absorbs the summer rain.

I have prayed
to the creator
for you
my nephew.

I have
humbled my soul

    so that I
    would have
    but a few moments
    in the place
    of the creators dwelling.

    For it will be you
    to seek a place
    for your children.

THE POWER WITHIN

My eyes
easily see
that which
I do see。

        but

              My mind
              can create

              and destroy

              just as easily。

Arise early.

Do not make yourself
a burden to the sun
for he carries the weight
of all who do not arise
when the morning comes.

Arise before he does

                    and greet him.

                    EXODUS

Upon
    the
        calm
            dry
                waves
                    of
                    the
                desert
            sea,
            the
            snake
                darts
                    forth
                        and
                    divides
                    the
                    sea,
                    and
                    flees
                        the
                        bondage
                            of t
                                    h
                                e s
                                        u
                                    n.

INHUMANITY

In the cool summer nights
that is sown upon the grass
I guard this realm with rapid rage
slicing twilight mass.

Being elusive, bold, and quick
I plunge forth as a sabre
I am a sentry of the night
a cavalier; my labor.

And as the day relieves me
I retreat to my lair
for tonight I return
to stab the cool night air.

My voice is not heard
as I fly in the night
but the hunters do listen
for the sound of my flight.

And though my pursuers
are frightened and weak
without understanding
my death do they seek.

Once I possessed
unyielding pride.
Now I'm slowly dying -
I'm being crucified.

They readied my dissection
for everyone to see
but these ungodly humans
would rather torture me!

BLACK MESA

black
winter
night
sky

stars
speckled
shining
suspended
in
universe

the
horizon
is
only
visible

when
the
orange
blast
of
dynamite

blows
out
another
chunk
of
mother
earth.

CLOUD BROTHERS

Four directions
cloud brothers
share one sky.

     Each has its own path.

     Each has its own mood.

     Each has its own face.

The cloud brothers are many
but they are one family.

The cloud brothers are scattered
but they are one spirit.

They mingle
within themselves

changing with every moment.

They tell us
that we too
are brothers
on this land.

And

like our cloud brothers

we are all yellow
          as are the sunrise clouds

we are all white
          as are the noonday clouds

we are all black
          as are the thunder clouds

we are all red
          as are the sunset clouds.

So let us look up to our cloud brothers
as one family
and one spirit.

For we   are truly different

and yet

    we   are truly the same.

EARTH MEADOW

In the valley
the flowers grow.

Blue

Yellow

They smile.

The sun warms
The earth nourishes.

A dragonfly rests.

Open your eyes
and look around you.

You too

are a flower

in the earth meadow.

ANTS

Silence is reflected upon the sky
for the blue haze is but a mirror.

I can feel
the subtleness of the breeze
and the silent fluttering of the moth.

A field of tall grass
sends a gentle wave of light
across the land.

It flows to eternity.

I gaze upon the ants
who toil for their children

for they do not consider
the lillies of the field.

A MOMENT BETWEEN DREAMS

Curled in bed
I gaze through tired eyes.
The luminous hands glow softly
and tell me   11:38

The sky is speckled with stars
and the spring breeze
quietly sneaks
through the wire window screens

All the while
I am lulled back to dreams
by an orchestra of frogs in the pond
and crickets in the fields.

MOON

moon   tell us when to plant our crops.
                tell us when to harvest our corn.

moon   command the coyotes to cry.
                command the rising of the tide.

moon   show us a different world.
                show us a respect for the night.

                Rise!

                pale orange

moon

                Rise!

FLOWER

As the morning mist
          descends

Green mountains become gray
                    then disappears.

The mountains
are swallowed.   They are helpless.

Below me

scattered patches of snowcrust
                    refuse to melt.

Dead pine needles
blanket the frozen ground.

I look up
at the merciless cold fog.

Then
I look down
in helpless anticipation

upon a small   purple

                    flower.

THE DAWN

Silently
the dawn creeps upon us.

The flowers stir
from the cool
swirling air.

Like a child
she slowly awakens
from dreams of stars
suspended in eternity
pulsating in space.

The creator
made the dawn to be a child-
one that is pure
and beautiful.
The stars were made
to be dreams-
mysterious
and eternal.

So
let us be thankful
for the dawn
and the stars.

For the dawn is a child

and the stars are eternal.

SONG OF THE HOER

Grime and sweat
running down
my forehead.
I feel it
running free
down my temples.

The muscles
in my arms
they suffer
from the weight
of my hoe
bearing down on

the roots of
the thistles
and bullheads.
The soft skin
on my neck
and shoulders turn

red and burn.
There is war
between me
and the weeds.
And it grows
year in ... year out.

So I know
the army
of the weeds
are legion.
But I have
as many days

before me.
Indeed, the
weeds are strong
and steadfast,
but I too
have strength, and a

sound weapon.
The weeds have
their allies;
the fieldmice,
the crows, the
heat of the sun.

But I have
the coolness
of the dawn
and the breeze
from the south.
It makes me sad

to think wars
are destined
and timeless,
having no
victories
and no defeats.

It saddens
me to think
that somewhere
battles are
always being
fought ... and every

day, one more
soldier dies.
So I must
admit my
weariness
and tiring

of this war.
On my way
home, I think.
If only
the weeds and
I could come to

understand
each other.
If only
I knew of
their purpose
and they, of mine.

But no. Wars
are destined
and timeless,
having no
victories
and no defeats.

This war of
mine will last
until I
die. And still
the weeds will
grow above me.

10;47 PM

I gaze up at
the night sky.

Taurus charges with unlimited fury!
and Saggitarius reels back in eager defense。

The moon rises
and separates their battle.

     They slowly fade into oblivion
     as the soft haze of the moon
     blends with the darkness.

I close my eyes   and wait.

The crickets surround me with song.
Gentle rain falls upon my face   then stops.

     And the warmth of the night
     puts me into a deep

          deep

        sleep.

THE PLACE

There is a place
hidden from most eyes.
I think of it often
for it is a part of me -
my soul
my existence.

When I am away
I think of it.
And in my sleep
I dream of it.

I dream of it.
This place
where life abounds
and makes known to me
that life is good.

I dream of it.
This place
where towering storm clouds
reveal unto me
their omnipotent powers;
where thunder roars out
from endless distances;
where lightning shares
but a moment of its existence
with mine.

I dream of it.
This place
where I
in contemplation
look into the granduer
of the crimson dawn
as it unfolds
into a brilliant amber;
where I behold
the coming of the day
as the forehead of the sun
slowly breaks over the horizon.

I dream of it.
This place
where the soft glowing flowers
reach up
for the warmth of the sun;
where the rabbits
as if elusive dolphins
skim the surface
of the desert sea.

I dream of it.
This place
where mine eyes
burn from my sweat
as I lay down seeds
into the moist earth;
where the red ants
climb upon me
and sting me;
where my strength
is taken from me
as the sun rises
to its zenith.
But I

I am content
and grateful
for all these things.

For this place
that I dream of

is my cornfield.

Where life abounds

and makes known to me

that life

is good.

BIRTH OF A SONG

A beautiful dawn has ascended.
Go   as you will
among the rows of corn.
With happy hearts
you will sing.
And once again
the clouds
will come forth
and rain。

Yes!
it is true
that from all directions
the clouds
will go among the cornfields
and nourish them
with moisture。

Yes!
it is true
my fathers
that the young corn
with happy hearts
will grow
and mature.

A beautiful dawn has ascended.
Go   as you will
among the rows of corn.
With happy hearts
you will sing。

CRICKET SOUNDS

To   sing my   song   forever I   go
    north   to   the yellow corn
to   sing   my song

        To sing   my   song   forever
I   go   west to the   blue
 corn   to sing   my   song

            to   sing my   song
for   ever I   go   south to
the   red   corn   to
   sing   my song

    to   sing   my song
forever   I go   east   to   the
    white   corn   to sing
  my song

I   sing   to   the sunrise
    I   sing   to the   sunset
  I   sing to the   sky   above

 I   sing   to   the ground
    below
I   sing to   life eternal
        I sing to life that is   past
    I   sing to life that is future
I   sing the   ETERNAL LIFE   song

To   sing   my song
    forever   I   will go
     to   all   directions
  to   sing my   song

SONG TO THE MOON

The moon rises
while stars fade.

Gray moon
slowly growing   night by night.

Expanding
as it feeds
on the darkness   of December

and sips
the sweet
comforting sounds   that fill the night.

Raise up your glass!

and taste
the smoothness
of the wind

rustling softly

                        through the sagebrush

and yonder
sparkling spring

                        running under your gaze.

Drink in   the crisp winter air.
Dine   on the serene reflection
                        of virgin snow.

For tomorrow
you shall be at your fullest.

COYOTE NIGHTS

Howling
under a full moon in July

    The coyotes

    who hide themselves
    in the wrinkled shadows
    of the sandstone cliffs

Sing out!

    and break the silence.

The vibrations of echo
fade out
and they howl once more.

    They are
    nature's gregorian chant

    and the universe
    is their cathedral.

WINTER NIGHT DANCES

Once again

winter night dances
wake the silent snow.

Once again

rattles are set in motion
mystic songs are sung
and vibrations become incessant.

Pot belly stoves
glow
red hot.

They sing a song
with the wind above.

Once again

winter night dances
wake the silent snow.

A SONG TO MY FATHERS

Yellow clouds appear

descending upon your fields.

They will go

among the rows

of the corn maidens

giving to them

soft rain.

This is what

you

my fathers

have prayed for.

THE GONER

The coyote knew
he was a goner.

Didn't even scream
when I cracked his skull

with the barrel
of my .410 shotgun.

My uncle and I
sent him back home

with some cornmeal
and bits of turquoise.

We threw him off
in the dry wash that runs by the road.

In the trash pile -
that is where we dumped his rotting carcass.

His pelt is drying
from the heat of the sun.

Bloodstained.

No big deal.

He was eating our unripe melons anyway.

ON THE EAST COAST

I have traveled very far
to the east
where the day begins.

Here I stand
face to face
with the Atlantic.

But my soul is filled with sadness
and my spirit longs to be back

      among the cliffs

      the fields

      the warm stone houses.

I miss the simple things like

      chopping wood for morning coffee

listening to the hiss of the coleman lantern

watching the bees caress the flowers.

And as I stand here
my heart cries out

      for the laughing child

      the mother of the child

      my home.

LIFE IN ITS ESSENCE

Yellow corn

        knowledge

Blue corn

        patience

Red corn

        respect

White corn

        purity

Corn is my life

    my existence

It is written   that man shall live

        by his own faith.

AFTER THE RAINS

Sandstone cliffs
reflect the red
of the setting sun.

My hoe is caked
with evidence
of my labor.

I see clouds
going to the east.
Dark clouds.

I look to the sky.
There!
A rainbow
is arched above me.

As I walk down
the dusty road
I look up.

Again!
The rainbow
dressed in beauty
walks with me.

There is no need
for us to speak.

Silence
will speak
for us.

CONTEMPLATING DEATH

(written at the Grand Canyon)

I look down
into the depths
of the canyon.

                    Wondering.

When shall I make my journey?
Who will be the first to greet me?
How long will I have to travel?
Where shall I begin?
What shall I say at my arrival?

Why?

                    I wonder.

Then
I say to myself

"Be patient"

The time will come
for you
to make the journey

THE RAVAGES OF AUTUMN

Autumn leaves
turning colors splendid.

They grapple
          hanging on for dear life

          spun around

          spun around

          by the constant blowing

                October wind.

They hang on
to long dead branches.

The wrinkled leaves grow weaker
               and weaker.

Someday soon
they will fall   and be carried
               by the wind

             free from suffering

                 at last.

IN CONTEMPLATION

Who are you
        that you would make the seed grow
                        make the eagle fly
        and make music flow like a river.

Who are you
        that you would give me breath of life
                        let my heart know love
        and let my mind know wisdom.

Who are you
        that you would make me smile
                        make me cry
        and make me wonder

    as I wonder about you

                        this moment.

WINTER SUNSET

standing
on mesa edge

I look far
into the gray horizon.
It is raining there.

The sandstone
is solid
and gritty
beneath my feet.

The movement of the wind
intensifies
and becomes more hostile
with every passing moment.

Minutes later.

Do the junipers
also sense
the sharp   cold   wind?

Or is it me
shaking and cold?

And my daughter says
"Daddy, let's go home."

A PSALM OF RAMSON

The sun is rising.
He rises.

In his turn
His rain bowed crown
Tells us of the coming rain.

Then
From all directions
The rains

They will descend
Softly
Upon our fields.

Selah

THOUGHTS

Tonight
I will dream of killing a rabbit.

Tomorrow
I will pray to see one.

Tomorrow
I will walk down the mesa.

Tonight
I will leave it up to the creator.

WORD PLAY

Can't write a poem in silence.

Just can't do it man
just can't do it.

Need something
need something now
need something to write 'bout.

Not the trees... not the flowers
can't think
can't think of nothin
let's see
let's see
whatdoIwriteabout?
I know!
Write about corn!
Corn?!
not corn!
not butterflies!
can't think
just can't think
just can't do it man!
just can't do it!
I'm goin nuts!
Crazy!
Yea!
That's it!
Crazy!
Nuts!
I'm goin nuts!
can't think!
can't think!
NO!
just can't think!
I know!
write 'bout Reagan!
jellybeans!
war!
budgets!
presidents!

Eisenhower!
Nixon!
Watergate!
investigate!
Pearly gate!
gateway to America!
America?!
YES!
America!
apple pie!
hot dogs!
SSSunday picnics!
free enterprise!
unemployment!
government!
B.I.A.!!!!!!!!!!!
reservation!
assimilation!
termination!
genocide!
injuns!
redskins!
Washington Redskins!
football!
whataboutfootball?!
Superbowl!
Rosebowl!
Cottonbowl!
Sugar bowl!
sacharrine bowl!
NO!
sacharrine causes cancer!
can't think!
can't think!
just can't think!
whatdoIwriteabout?!
hunger?!
sadness?!
WHAT?!
tell me...WHAT?!
I don't know!
my pencil's dumb!
NO!
it's me!
it's me!

I'm dumb!
I'mtheonethatscrazy!
can't think!
can't think!
just can't think!
Custer died for your sins!
he died!
he died!
YES!
he died!
Custer died for your sins!
don't 'cha know?!
he died!
Lincoln died!
Moses died!
babies died!
M'daddy died!
I died!
I died!
cuz I can't think!
But my pencils movin!
Cuz it's alive!
the pencils alive!
the hills are alive!
the hills are alive!
the hills are alive!
with the sound of bombs!
guns!
but not music!
bombs!
guns!
and congressional hearings!
That's WAR!!!
civil war!
cold war!
generals!
colonels!
corn kernals!
Kentuckey fried colonels!
That's right!
WARS!!!
can't think!
can't think!
just can't think!
Nobody thinks!

```
YES!
nobody thinks!
nobody sez pleez!
nobody sez thank you!
nobody sez nothin'!
cuz we can't think!
cuz we don't think!
you don't think!
I don't think!
all God's children don't think!
can't think!
can't think!
just can't think!
```

Can't write a poem in silence.

Just can't do it man
just can't do it.

A PRAYER IN NEW ENGLAND

I am alone
yet
in the presence of the creator.
I feel the creation force that surrounds me.
I am   a part of it.

Hear me, you who stands alone.
I have come to talk.
Be at peace, for I come with a humble heart.
I am one among you.

Spruce trees
you are strong
you are quiet
your branches   outstretched.
the clouds rest on your branches.

I am I
a part of nature
a part of your creation.
Hear me. You   who guides the life path.
Let the spruce trees bear witness.

I ask for wisdom
for the sake of our children.
I ask for guidance
for the sake of mine own.
Lead me in the days to come.

For I am I.

Your servant.